MW01097747

Expecting You

My Pregnancy Journal

LINDA KRANZ   photographs by KLAUS KRANZ

Da Capo
∞
LIFE
LONG

A Member of the Perseus Books Group

Many of the designations used by manufactures and sellers to distinguish their products are claimed as trademarks. Where those designations appear in this book and Da Capo Press was aware of a trademark. Where those designations appear in this book and Da Capo Press was aware of a trademark claim, the designations have been printed in initial capital letters.

Copyright © 2000 by Linda Kranz and Klaus Kranz

All rights reserved. No part of this publication may be reproduced, stored in a retrieval system, or transmitted, in any form or by any means, electronic, mechanical, photocopying, recording, or otherwise, without the prior written permission of the publisher. Printed in the United States of America.

Library of Congress Cataloging-in-Publication Data
Kranz, Linda.
    Expecting you: my pregnancy journal / Linda Kranz; photographs by Klaus Kranz.
       p.   cm.
    ISBN-13 978-1-55561-245-0   ISBN-10 1-55561-245-8
    1. Pregnancy—Popular works. 2. Pregnancy—Miscellanea. I. Kranz, Klaus. II. Title.

RG525 .K736 2000
618.2'4—dc21   00-034793

www.dacapopress.com

Da Capo Press books are available at special discounts for bulk purchases in the United States by corporations, institutions, and other organizations. For more information, please contact the Special Markets Department at the Perseus Books Group, 11 Cambridge Center, Cambridge, MA 02142, or call (800) 255-1514 or (617) 252-5298 or e-mail Special.Markets@perseusbooks.com

Text design by Billie Jo Bishop
Cover design by Billie Jo Bishop
Cover photography by Klaus Kranz

Thermometer image appearing on page 47 and 116 © Eyewire, Inc.

10 DHSB 12 11 10 9

This journal belongs to

_____

I started this journal on ____/____/____,

in the city of _____,

in the state of _____,

when I was _____ years old.

My due date is ____/____/____.

This is about my pregnancy with _____,

who was born _____ in the year _____ at ___:___ A.M. / P.M.
          MONTH / DAY

This journal was given to me by

_____

Also by LINDA KRANZ

For My Child: A Mother's Keepsake Journal
A Father's Journal: Memories for My Child
All about Me: A Keepsake Journal for Kids
More about Me: Another Keepsake Journal for Kids
Through My Eyes: A Journal for Teens

For my parents, Jayne and Bill, thank you for me.

For my dear friends Gloria and Gloria,
mothers extraordinaire!

And for all mothers-to-be, as you wait for the

 arrival of your child. Be kind

to yourself. Slow your pace a little and

prepare to hold in your arms a true miracle.

Your life will be forever changed.

Introduction

CONGRATULATIONS! You must be excited. When I found out I was expecting, I couldn't seem to stop smiling. I remember thinking I had this wonderful secret because I wasn't showing yet. I couldn't wait to share the news with the world.

A year or so before I became pregnant with our daughter, I found a pregnancy journal in a small gift shop. I bought it and put it away in a closet. The day I found out I was expecting, I pulled down the journal from the shelf and filled the first page. I continued to fill the pages as the weeks and months went by. I wrote down notes about doctor's visits, what I was eating, and thoughts about the way I was feeling.

Five years later, when I was carrying our son, I bought another journal, to capture my thoughts again. I'm so glad I wrote down everything that I was experiencing. I have re-read those journals many times over the last several years. Whenever I read them I'm transported back to that time, as if it were just yesterday.

Putting together this journal brought back all kinds of memories. As Klaus and I gathered items to photograph, spoke to new parents and even attended a childbirth-education class, we found that being in a room filled with first- and second-time parents brought back the same excitement we had felt ourselves during my pregnancies. I smiled at my husband across the room as he photographed them. They practiced their short hee-hee breaths and cleansing breaths, they watched a video and lay on the floor with their pillows and blankets and hugged like spoons. They listened to relaxing music with the lights down low. The childbirth instructor emphasized to the couples to make the most of this time. "When the baby comes," she said, "life changes. Allow time for yourselves." Good advice. Something to take to heart whether your children are newborns or in their teens. Make time for you to share and enjoy each other as a couple.

Since becoming a mother, I often find myself thinking about my own childhood. I wonder what life was like for my parents when they were expecting me: how they handled certain situations, what was important to them. I think about how life changes from one generation to the next and how in many ways it stays the same.

About This Journal

When I began to think about questions to include on these pages, I looked at my own two journals, and I expanded the ideas I was asked to write about. Over the years, I have become a journal writer. I believe that with the right focus you can capture what is going on in your life beyond the basic doctor visits and bouts of morning sickness to capture what is truly important to you. And years from now, your children and your children's children will delight at reading every word that you had to say. We are all in the process of making history.

After you've completed this journal, tuck it away with photos and mementos from this special event. Years down the road, when you happen on it again, I'm sure you will savor re-reading each page. When you have finished, once again put away the journal, until your child, to whom you so carefully wrote your story, becomes a parent. That's when this journal will be appreciated again and will be read with great interest.

I hope you enjoy this process. I have given you topics to get you started. If you come across a question that you don't have an answer for, cross it out and write down the thoughts you want to capture there. This journal is to be used in a very flexible way. Be sure to date all of your responses. You can answer many of the questions more than once as the months go by and your perspective changes.

Journaling is relaxing. Right now, you are experiencing many different emotions. One minute you are happy, and hours later you may be worrying about something. Some days fly by, others move at a snail's pace. What better time to pull out this journal and record in your own handwriting what you are thinking.

What a wonderful keepsake for your family! I know you will enjoy filling up these pages. So pick up your pen and begin to write. Have fun and once more . . . CONGRATULATIONS!

Happiness,

Linda

LINDA KRANZ

Expecting You

I have wanted to be a mother since . . .

I first suspected
that I was
pregnant
because . . .
I found out I
was indeed
expecting on
___ / ___ / ___ .
My reaction
was . . .

If I were to describe your father,

this is what I would say . . .

How I met your father.

....

....

....

....

....

....   WHAT I SAW IN HIM

....   THAT MADE ME

....   WANT TO GET TO

....   KNOW HIM BETTER.

....   OUR FIRST KISS,

....   OUR FIRST EMBRACE.

....

....

....

....

....

....

....

....

....

....

....

....

The way I broke
the news to
your father.

His reaction.
Highlights of that
day and
evening.

Other reactions from loved ones, friends and co-workers.

What I know about my own birth.

....

....

....

....

Where I was born.
The year.
The day of the week,
the time and
how much I weighed.
How old my parents
were when I was born.
What they did
for a living.
This is how my mom
describes that day
in her own words.
Or how a relative or
close friend of the family
remembers that day.

....

....

....

....

....

....

....

....

....

....

....

....

....

....

....

....

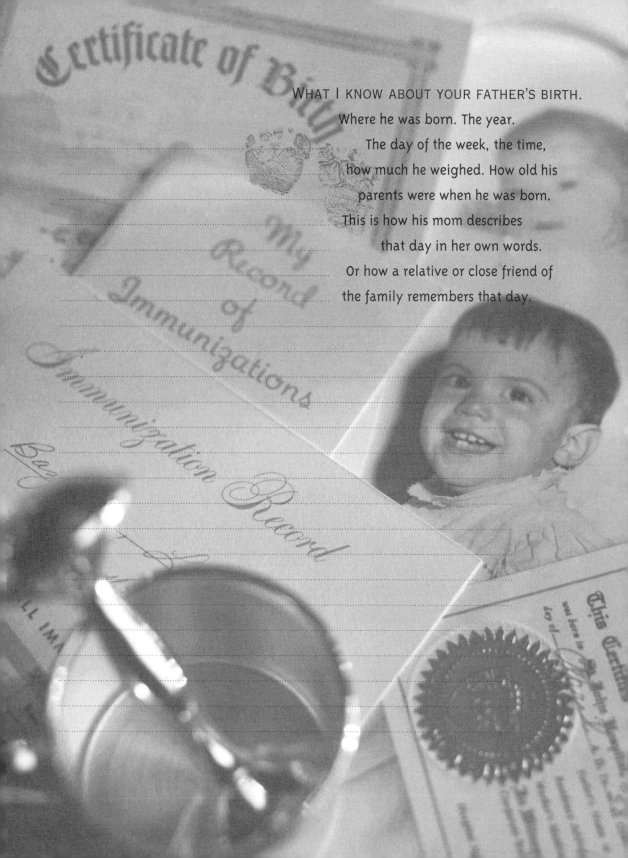

WHAT I KNOW ABOUT YOUR FATHER'S BIRTH.
Where he was born. The year.
The day of the week, the time,
how much he weighed. How old his
parents were when he was born.
This is how his mom describes
that day in her own words.
Or how a relative or close friend of
the family remembers that day.

MY DOCTOR'S NAME.

How and why I chose
my doctor or midwife.
The fee he or she charges.
The office is close by or
miles from our home.

Now that I've had some time to think about being pregnant, these are my thoughts, concerns and how I'm feeling right now.

When I first learned
    that I was pregnant,
the following trends,
fashions and
    newsworthy events
were happening
    around the world
and close by.

MY FIRST DOCTOR'S APPOINTMENT WAS TODAY, ___/___/___.

I'M ___ WEEKS PREGNANT. WHAT WE TALKED ABOUT.

HOW MUCH I WEIGH.

How I would describe myself.
My likes and dislikes.
My temperament and appearance.
If someone were to read this description,
they would recognize me.

Write more thoughts on this page.

Listen to friends and co-workers about memories of their pregnancies, but realize that each person's experiences are unique. You may not have the same experiences.

Set aside time to do nothing. Watch clouds float by on a sunny afternoon, read a book or take a quiet walk. Enjoy this time. Relax.

Everyone has dreams. These are mine.

MY FAVORITE TIME OF THE DAY.

HOW I SPEND MY EVENINGS.

What's going on
      in my life right now.
Things that matter
      most to me.

How I've been feeling.
Bouts with morning sickness
or headaches. My energy level.

I HOPE YOU WILL INHERIT THESE TRAITS FROM ME.

I HOPE YOU WILL INHERIT THESE TRAITS FROM YOUR FATHER.

$\mathcal{N}$ow that I'm
expecting you,
these are the things
I notice
around me that
I never paid attention
to before.

A typical day that I've had lately.

Today's date:
___/___/___.
My changing
emotions,
how I am dealing
with them.

FOODS I CRAVE.

Foods I used to love
but that I can't
      eat any more.
Our favorite foods
      for dinner.
Favorite recipes.
  My cooking skills.
Who does most of
      the cooking.
A typical week's
menu right now
      consists of . . .

I HAD A DOCTOR'S
APPOINTMENT
TODAY, ___/___/___.
I'M ___ WEEKS
PREGNANT. WHAT WE
DISCUSSED. HOW
MUCH I WEIGH.

My thoughts when
  I heard your heart beat
for the first time.
  I was ___ weeks
      pregnant.

Write more thoughts on this page.

Enjoy each day of your pregnancy.

Years from now, when you think back

to this time, you will smile.

The best gifts you can offer your children

are a loving home,

a listening ear, a warm smile

and a hand to hold

when they reach out to you.

WINTER, SPRING,
   SUMMER
      OR FALL.
Which seasons I will
experience as
      I carry you.
My favorite season
      of the year.

TIMES WHEN I FELT PHYSICALLY AND MENTALLY EXHAUSTED, YET I KEPT GOING. WHAT HELPED ME KEEP GOING. WAYS I'VE FOUND TO RECHARGE.

What I am thankful for . . .

....
....
....
....
....
....
....
....
....
....
....
....
....
....
....
....
....
....
....
....
....
....
....
....
....
....
....
....

ABOUT THE TOWN WE LIVE IN.

What brought us here. What I like about it. Changes I've noticed in the time that we have lived here.

On this page I will
write compliments
I have received,
so whenever
I'm feeling blue,
I can turn to this
page and smile.

BOOKS I'VE BEEN READING ABOUT PREGNANCY.

My favorites, which I would recommend to others.

What I've learned from them.

A few goals
I have achieved and
others I am working on
for the future.

AFTER THE BILLS ARE PAID
and there's a little
extra cash left,
this is what
I like to spend
the money on . . .

*Thoughts and memories
I want to share
with you about your
grandparents.*

IN MY FAMILY
I WAS THE OLDEST,
MIDDLE, YOUNGEST OR
AN ONLY CHILD.
SOME OF MY FAVORITE
MEMORIES FROM WHEN
I WAS GROWING UP.

Other family stories I want to share with you.

Experiences I hope you will have as you grow up.

Holidays I will celebrate

while I'm carrying you.
My favorite holiday.
Why it's special to me.

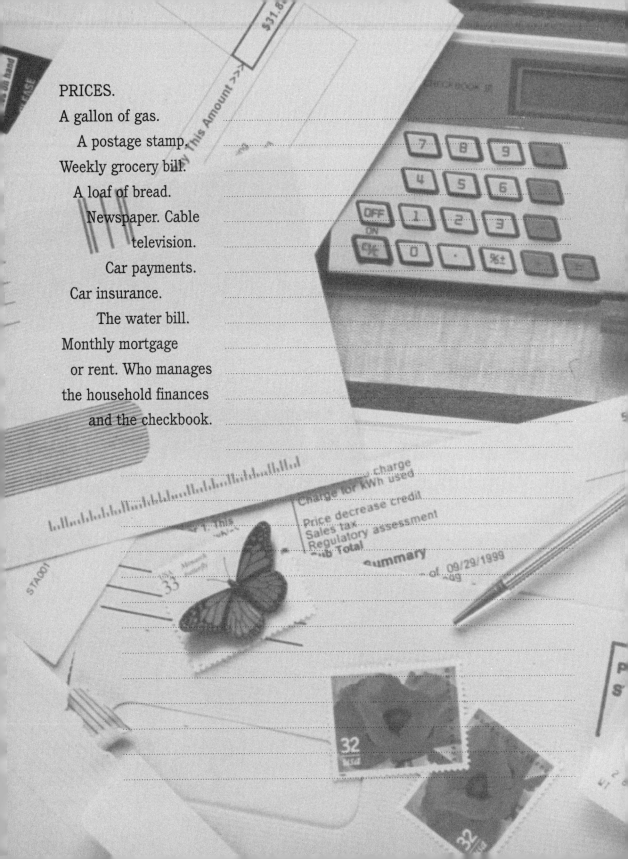

PRICES.
A gallon of gas.
   A postage stamp.
Weekly grocery bill.
   A loaf of bread.
      Newspaper. Cable
         television.
      Car payments.
Car insurance.
      The water bill.
Monthly mortgage
   or rent. Who manages
the household finances
   and the checkbook.

....

....

....

....

....

....

....

....   HOW YOUR FATHER

....   AND I LIKE TO

....   SPEND TIME TOGETHER.

....   WAYS WE

....   COMPLEMENT

....   EACH OTHER.

....

....

....

....

....

....

....

....

....

....

....

*Some of my
most prized
possessions are . . .
Why they
are so special.*

A funny moment that
happened during
my pregnancy.
Who was involved,
what happened
and why it
made me laugh.

BAD HABITS I'VE
DEVELOPED OVER THE
YEARS, WHICH I
    GAVE UP WHEN I
FOUND OUT I WAS
EXPECTING YOU.
GOOD HABITS I HAVE
    INCORPORATED INTO MY
DAILY ROUTINE NOW.

Exercise.

Drink plenty of water every day.

Get as much rest as possible.

Eat nutritiously, especially lots of

fruits and vegetables.

Take a pregnancy vitamin

as your doctor suggests.

I had a doctor's appointment today, ___/___/___.

....
....
....
....
....

I'm ___ weeks
pregnant.
What we discussed.
How much I weigh.
(Take a photo as
your pregnancy starts
to show to include in
your journal.)

The ideal age to
become a parent is . . .
Why I feel this way.
Observations I've
made about family
and friends when they
became parents.

If I were to compare how childbirth and rearing a family
has changed from my parents' generation, I would say . . .

....

....

....

....

....

....

....

....

....

....

....

....

....

....

....

....

....

....

....

....

....

....

WHAT MAKES ME HAPPY.
IF SOMEONE ASKED WHAT
MY PRESCRIPTION FOR HAPPINESS IS,
I WOULD SAY . . .

A four-leaf clover,
   a rainbow after a storm,
a fortune cookie,
   a heads-up penny,
my horoscope . . .
What these things
   mean to me.

My talents.
Hobbies that I enjoy. ....

....

....

....

....

....

....

....

....

....

....

....

....

....

....

....

....

....

The kind of
car I drive.
Why I chose it.
If I could buy another car,
the one I have
my eye on is . . .
Why I like it.

The first items we
bought for you were
(clothes, toys or
other items) . . .
Thoughts as we
were shopping.

....

....

....

....

....

....

....

....

....

....

....

....

....

....

....

....

IF I COULD CHANGE THE WORLD, THIS IS WHAT I WOULD DO . . .

Inventions or products you will have as you grow up that my generation didn't have.

Ways your father has made
this pregnancy more
comfortable for me.
Times when he
truly surprised me.

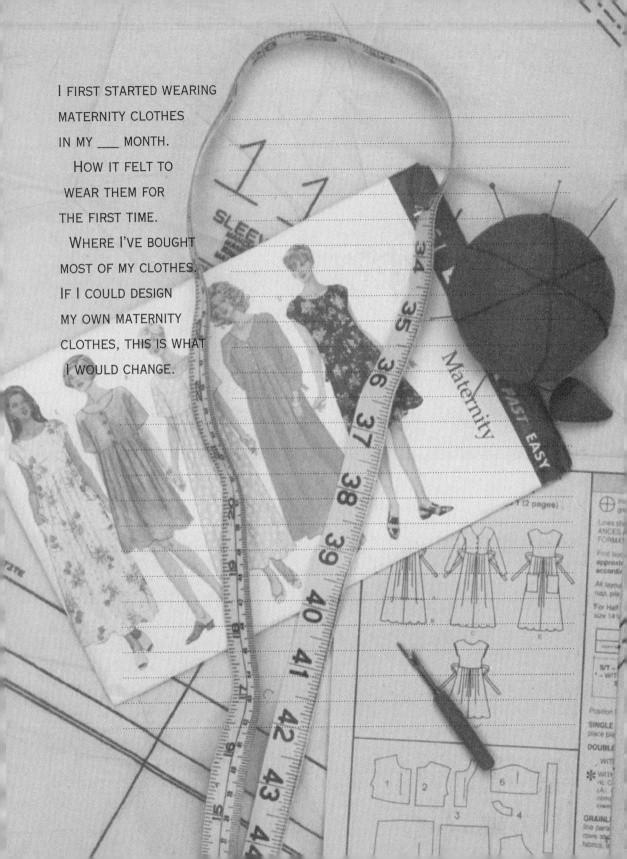

I FIRST STARTED WEARING
MATERNITY CLOTHES
IN MY ___ MONTH.
　　HOW IT FELT TO
WEAR THEM FOR
THE FIRST TIME.
　　WHERE I'VE BOUGHT
MOST OF MY CLOTHES.
IF I COULD DESIGN
MY OWN MATERNITY
CLOTHES, THIS IS WHAT
I WOULD CHANGE.

People I've called
or talked to for
advice during
this pregnancy.
Ways they have
helped me.

I had a doctor's appointment today, ___/___/___.
I'm ___ weeks pregnant.
What we discussed. How much I weigh.

What the weather
is like.
Today's date is
__/__/__.
My comfort level
right now is . . .

*How we spend
our weekends.*

What time we get up.

What we enjoy doing.

Becoming a mother means the focus shifts

from thinking of "me first" to thinking of

"my child" first. This shift happens naturally.

As our children grow,

we do our best to instill good qualities

that will carry them through life.

You know you have succeeded when

your children say in their own words

those things that you have been saying

all along.

A FEW
MOTHERS
I ADMIRE.
These are a few of
the qualities I've noticed
in them that I want to
carry into motherhood.
Why I think I'll be
a great mother.

....

....

....

....

....

....

....

....

....   *Things I plan to do with*

....   *my family that are*

....   *different or the same*

....   *as my parents did when*

....   *they reared me.*

....

....

....

....

....

....

....

....

....

....

....

My favorite fragrance, color, flower, sound.

I wanted to write this down so I wouldn't forget it.

How I would like to leave
my mark on the world.

People I admire
whom I've met or
with whom I work.
Famous people who
inspire me to reach
for something more.
What I see in them.

The first time I felt you move was ___/___/___.

You seem to be
the most active during
the morning, afternoon,
evening or when
I lie down for bed.
Hiccups, somersaults
and other movements
you make.

Here I will trace my hand.

I CAN REST
MY HANDS ON MY
STOMACH AND
FEEL YOU MOVE.
WHEN YOU ARE
A NEWBORN,
JUST HOME FROM
THE HOSPITAL,
I WILL TRACE
YOUR HAND
INSIDE OF THE
TRACING OF
MY HAND.

What I think about
   before I drift off to sleep.

People in my life
who have helped me
become the person
I am today.

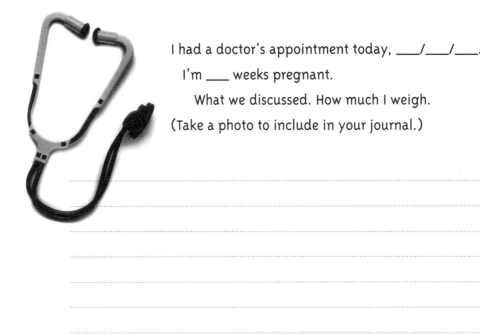

I had a doctor's appointment today, ___/___/___.

I'm ___ weeks pregnant.

What we discussed. How much I weigh.

(Take a photo to include in your journal.)

SOME CHANGES IN
YOUR FATHER'S AND
MY RELATIONSHIP
THAT I'VE NOTICED
DURING THIS
PREGNANCY.

Current events.
The names of the
President
      and Vice-President.
Discoveries in science
   I heard about this
year, and why they are
considered important.

Pets.

THEIR NAMES.

HOW WE FOUND THEM.

HOW LONG WE

HAVE HAD THEM.

CHANGES I FORESEE

WHEN YOU ARE BORN.

Favorite quotations that have stayed with me
and inspired me over the years.

"

VACATIONS OR
WEEKEND GETAWAYS
WHILE I WAS
EXPECTING. WHERE WE
WENT. WHAT IT WAS
LIKE.

The career I have chosen. Ways that it suits me. Or a career I hope to pursue in the future.

Your father's career. How he chose it. Some hopes he has for the future.

Books I've read recently that I've enjoyed. Favorite authors.

MOVIES I'VE SEEN
recently that I've
enjoyed. Favorite
actors. Television shows
that your father and I
watch together. Videos
I could watch again
and again.
The messages I like in
my favorite movies.

WOOD
UCTION
TOR
ERA
TE   SCENE   TAKE

WHEN I LOOK IN THE MIRROR, THIS IS WHAT I SEE.

TODAY'S DATE: ___/___/___.

Our home.

The address. Why we chose this neighborhood over others.

How I would describe it. What I like about it.

....
....
....
....
....
....
....
....
....
....
....
....
....
....
....
....
....
....

HOW WE HAVE
FURNISHED OUR HOME.
WALL HANGINGS.
THE COLORS WE USED.
WHAT I SEE OUT OUR
LIVING ROOM WINDOW.
WHAT OUR BACKYARD IS
LIKE. HOW WE SHARE
HOUSEHOLD CHORES.
HOUSE-CLEANING TIPS.

If I wanted time alone to think,

this is where I would go.

WHEN YOU
ARE BORN,
I LOOK FORWARD
TO THESE THINGS . . .

If I had a reason
to celebrate and
wanted to treat myself,
I would do this . . .

*"There are no coincidences;
everything happens for a reason."*

How I feel about this saying.

....
....
....
....
....
....
....
....
....
....
....
....
....
....
....
....
....
....
....
....
....
....

I had a doctor's
appointment today,
___/___/___.
I'm ___ weeks
pregnant.
What we discussed.
How much
I weigh.

Shower your child with love.

Be understanding and patient.

Children learn about relationships

and how to love by our example.

From board books to picture books to

chapter books, let reading become part of

your daily ritual with your child.

What a wonderful activity to share!

I've decided to breastfeed or bottle-feed and these are my reasons for this choice.

Ways I've found to be active
and exercise. How I feel
before I exercise and
afterward. Why I like it
or why it is hard for me.

Family members who have helped during my pregnancy.

Dreams I've
        been having that
I remember
        so clearly.

My tour of the hospital.

WHAT I NOTICED.
CHILDBIRTH CLASSES.
WHEN WE STARTED.
HOW LONG
    THEY LASTED.
WHAT WE LEARNED.
    WHAT MY
INSTRUCTOR IS LIKE.

What we are
doing to prepare
for your
homecoming.
Your room.
How we are
decorating it.

A typical day that
  I've had lately.
Today's date:
  ___/___/___.
My changing emotions
and how I am dealing
  with them.

My sleep habits.
How they are changing.
When I have trouble
sleeping, I . . .

A TIME I WAS
WORRIED OR SCARED
DURING THIS
PREGNANCY.
HOW I DEALT WITH
MY FEELINGS AND HOW
THINGS TURNED OUT.

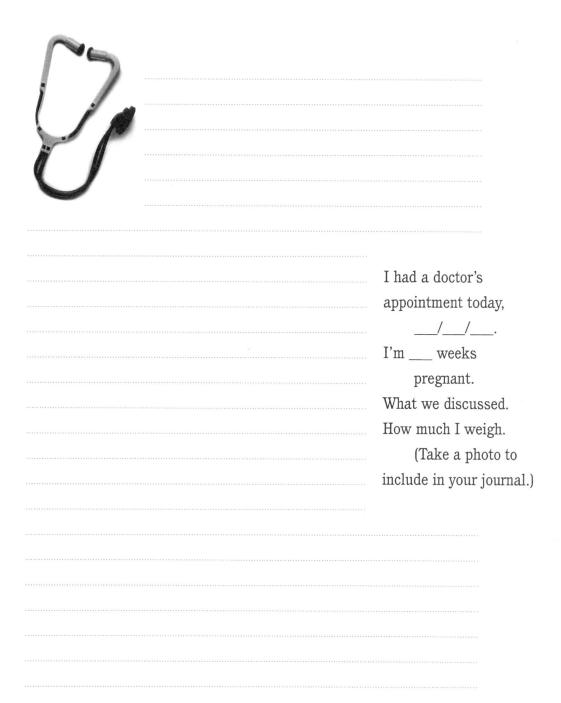

I had a doctor's
appointment today,
___/___/___.
I'm ___ weeks
    pregnant.
What we discussed.
How much I weigh.
    (Take a photo to
include in your journal.)

Music I listen to right now. The artists and the names of the songs. When I hear these songs, I will think about this special time, when I was expecting you.

Traditions I want for our family.

MILESTONES, EVENTS
AND RITES OF PASSAGE
I LOOK FORWARD TO
SHARING WITH YOU.

A family member
    who will come to
stay with us after you
are born.
    Someone I wish
        could come, but
it's not possible for
him or her to make it.

*Where I see our
family five years
from now.*

The ideal number of
years between siblings,
I think, is . . .
How your siblings are
reacting to the idea
of having a new
brother or sister.
Ways we are involving
them in this event.

IF GIVEN THE CHOICE
TO FIND OUT
IF YOU ARE A BOY
OR A GIRL, I WILL SAY
"YES," OR I WILL SAY
"NO" AND BE
SURPRISED. WHY I FEEL
THIS WAY.

I had a doctor's
appointment today,
___ / ___ / ___.
I'm ___ weeks pregnant.
What we discussed.
How much I weigh.

How far
the hospital is
from our house.
The name of the
hospital.
The route we have
planned. Or our
midwife lives about
___ minutes from
our home.

I had a doctor's appointment today, ___/___/___.
I'm ___ weeks pregnant. What we discussed. My weight.

WAYS I'VE FOUND TO BE COMFORTABLE,

  NOW THAT MY DUE DATE ISN'T FAR AWAY.

  AN EXAMPLE OF A TIME WHEN I REALLY

    FELT PREGNANT. THINGS I CAN'T DO ON MY OWN ANYMORE, SUCH AS TIE MY SHOES OR GET DRESSED. I NEED

    HELP WHEN I . . .

Write more thoughts on this page.

Children don't ask to be born.

They are created out of a strong love

between two people, and that blending

is evident in the child that

you have together.

All along, it's been two of you,

and now you've become three.

A family is born along with this child.

My baby shower.
Who arranged it.
Friends and loved ones
who attended.
Special moments
I won't forget.
Gifts I received.

Physical changes I've noticed
through the months.

I HAD A DOCTOR'S
APPOINTMENT
TODAY, ___/___/___.
I'M ___ WEEKS PREGNANT.
WHAT WE DISCUSSED.
HOW MUCH I WEIGH.
(TAKE A PHOTO TO
INCLUDE IN
YOUR JOURNAL.)

MY SUITCASE

for the hospital is ready.
I finished packing today,
___/___/___.
Here's what I packed . . .

Where I was and what time of day it was when labor started. Who was with me. I knew it was time to go to the hospital or call my midwife when . . .

WHAT I REMEMBER
ABOUT THE RIDE.
WHAT TIME WE GOT
TO THE HOSPITAL.
WHO GREETED US.
OR, HOW I WAS
FEELING WHEN
THE MIDWIFE ARRIVED.

My memories of labor.

How long it lasted.
My doctor's or midwife's
bedside manner.
Nurses or family members
who helped me.
Those who made a big
difference to my mood
and comfort.

How your father participated
and "held up" through labor.

....
....
....
....
....
....
....
....
....
....
....
....
....
....
....
....
....
....
....
....
....
....
....

The first time I saw you
and held you.
My thoughts and
feelings.
Your father's reaction
when he saw you.

Your name.

....

....

....

....

....

....

....

....

....

....

....

....

....

....

....

....

....

....

....

....

....

....

OTHER NAMES WE
CONSIDERED. I READ
SELECTIONS FROM
COUNTLESS BABY-
NAME BOOKS ALOUD
EACH NIGHT. WE
HAD IT CHOSEN
FOR YEARS, OR WE
WAITED UNTIL
WE SAW YOU, AND
THAT'S WHEN WE
KNEW WHAT YOUR
NAME WOULD BE.
HOW YOUR DAD
AND I FEEL ABOUT
OUR NAMES.

lan ALEX *Alexis* BARBAR
Alicia AMETHYS
ART BERNADETTE *Byron* Brya
Allison B r y a n **Abbey ben**
Brittany Aaron

The first person
we called to say
our baby had
arrived was . . .
Other people
we called.

The ride home from the hospital.
Our first night at home; what it was like.

Baby
on
Board

....

....

....

....

....

....

....

....

....

....

....

....

....

....

....

....

....

....

....

....

Special phone calls,
letters, cards, visits from
friends and family.

Your little footprints.

YOU ARE ___ DAYS OLD. HERE IS THE NEWSPAPER CLIPPING ANNOUNCING YOUR BIRTH.

Feeding time, changing diapers,
sponge-bathing you.
This was what our
first week home was like.

My reflections of
pregnancy,
* birth and*
becoming a parent.

When your
umbilical cord
fell off.
  What you
thought of your
first official
  bath.

ADVICE I WOULD GIVE TO ANOTHER EXPECTANT MOTHER NOW THAT I HAVE CARRIED AND DELIVERED A CHILD.

....

....

....

....

....

....

....

....

....

....

....

....

....

....

....

....

....

....

....

....

....

....

....

....

My hopes and wishes for you.

About the Author and Photographer

LINDA AND KLAUS met when her father was stationed overseas—they were fourteen and fifteen years old. Two weeks after this manuscript was due to the publisher, they celebrated their twenty-sixth wedding anniversary. This year they will celebrate their thirty-fifth wedding anniversary. They have two grown children, Jessica and Nik. As parents Klaus and Linda enjoyed watching and guiding their children through their childhood and teen years. Linda says that as a mother she often referred to the journal she started keeping at age twelve, which reminded her of what she experienced as a teen. "Journals make sure we remember important aspects of our lives."

Klaus's photography has appeared on book covers, note cards, inside books and in magazines. Linda is the author of eight journals, a rock painting book for kids, and most recently a children's book titled *Only One You.* You can see a complete listing of the books Linda has authored on her Web site. www.lindakranz.com.

There's a saying: "Feedback is the spice of life." We would love to hear from you, please write to us at:

Linda and Klaus Kranz

P.O. Box 2404

Flagstaff, AZ 86003-2404

Or you can email me at linda@lindakranz.com